For Keiran Maye and other boys who
like reading (and those who don't)
N. D.

For Ben, the graphic communicator!
N. L.

Text copyright © 2011 by Nicola Davies
Illustrations copyright © 2011 by Neal Layton

First U.S. edition 2011

Library of Congress Cataloging-in-Publication Data
Davies, Nicola, date.
Talk talk squawk : a human's guide to animal communication / Nicola Davies ; illustrated by Neal Layton.
p.   cm.
ISBN 978-0-7636-5088-9
1. Animal communication. 2. Human-animal communication. 3. Human-animal relationships. I. Title.
QL776.D376 2011
591.59—dc22   2010040794

SCP 16 15 14 13 12 11
10 9 8 7 6 5 4 3 2 1

Printed in Humen, Dongguan, China

This book was typeset in AT Arta. The illustrations were done in ink and digitally colored.

Candlewick Press, 99 Dover Street, Somerville, Massachusetts 02144

visit us at www.candlewick.com

THE PANDA ON
THE OPPOSITE PAGE IS DOING
A HANDSTAND AGAINST A TREE.
YOU CAN FIND OUT WHY IF YOU TURN TO PAGE 20.

Talk, Talk, Squawk!

A Human's Guide to Animal Communication

Nicola Davies

illustrated by **Neal Layton**

CANDLEWICK PRESS

Human beings never
stop communicating!

With words . . .

with faces . . .

6

with hands . . .

**not to mention with signs,
signals, flashing lights,
and sirens.**

And we aren't the only ones. . . .

Wherever you go on the planet, animals are doing it, too!

In African jungles, putty-nosed monkeys use sounds just like words: *pyow* means "leopard," *hack* means "eagle," and putting the two together, *pyow-hack* means "Let's go!"

PYOW!

HACK!

PYOW-HACK!

Stinkbugs in parks and gardens tap out messages on leaves and branches so that they can find one another.

TAP TAP TAP TAP

FOOD THIS WAY

Parasol ants in South American rain forests lay scent trails that act like direction signs, showing other ants the way to the nearest food.

In American woodlands, red-eyed vireos sing from dawn to dusk. Each male will sing as many as 22,000 times a day to tell other vireos to keep out of his territory.

Far out in the ocean, blue whales use deep hums as loud as an airplane taking off to send messages across hundreds of miles of ocean.

In the murky water of African rivers, elephant-nose fish use electric pulses to send signals that say "I'm the boss."

On coral reefs, the bright colors and patterns of different species of butterfly fish are like labels saying what kind of fish they are.

HUM! HUM! HUM! HUM! hum!

Communicate or Perish!

It's clear from all the singing, tapping, buzzing, humming, flashing, and howling going on that communication is as important to animals as it is to us. In fact, almost all the things that animals do — like finding food and shelter, meeting a mate, and rearing young — would be impossible without it. Every animal has to communicate in some way.

Good communication means animals have to send signals that the animals on the receiving end are going to be able to sense and understand. For instance, it's no good whispering in the middle of a thunderstorm, flashing a light to attract a mate if that mate is blind, or waving a white flag if the enemy thinks that the sign of surrender is a blue flag. No one wins if communication is confusing!

So animals have come up with ways to make signals that work even when it's too dark to see, too noisy to hear, or the animal they're trying to reach is a hundred miles away or even a member of a different species.

11

Uniforms

Uniforms are a very simple type of signal that says "one of us." Even the ugliest uniform — like the purple and yellow striped blazer I had to wear to school — is a really useful way to spot your friends in a crowd.

This bright colors and patterns of butterfly fish work the same way, "labeling" the fish so that they can find their friends fast. There can be several different kinds of butterfly fish living on the same piece of coral reef, and no fish wants to waste time courting a member of another species, so they all have a different "uniform," colors and patterns that are particular to each species, the way my ugly blazer was particular to my school.

12

Butterfly
Fish

BUTTERFLY
FISH HIGH
SCHOOL

Many other kinds of animals use such markings to help them to pick out members of their own species. Guenons are a family of monkeys that live in the forests of Africa. They have striking facial patterns that allow them to find members of their own species when several different kinds of monkey are feeding in the same area of forest or even in the same tree.

Uniforms not only tell you who's on your team; they can also tell you what jobs everyone does. How would you tell the cops from the robbers if they all wore jeans and T-shirts?

Cleaner wrasse are little reef fish that make their living by, you guessed it, cleaning. They pick tiny parasitic creatures from the skins of much larger reef-living creatures and eat them. This job requires trust on both sides: the wrasse must trust their big customers not to make a meal of them, and their customers must trust the wrasse not to take a mouthful of tender skin. So the wrasse signal that they are not just any old fish out for a quick meal by "wearing a uniform": their bodies are colored with neat black and blue stripes that make them look quite different from any other fish. To make doubly certain their customers know who they are, they do a little dance, wiggling their bodies back and forth in the water.

Stripes Spell Danger

There's one kind of animal "uniform" that sends a signal that's understood even by humans: bright colors or bold stripes spell "danger." Many small animals use this signal to tell the world that they are not a tasty meal!

The bold yellow and black stripes of bees and wasps remind predators that they carry a painful sting. Cinnabar moth caterpillars are packed with poisons from the plants they eat, so to birds their orange and black pattern says "Yuck!" Coral snakes warn of their lethal bite with red, yellow, and black stripes, and tiny poison arrow frogs, whose skins carry deadly toxins, are colored like bright jewels.

Why go to the trouble of being bright and stripy if you already have a nasty bite, sting, or taste to keep predators at bay? Well, firstly, bright colors stand out, keeping you from getting eaten by mistake by a predator who didn't see you or thought you were ordinary yummy prey. Secondly, having a color and pattern similar to other kinds of inedible or poisonous animals means that the predator may already have learned what your pattern means without having to taste you to find out.

A danger signal like this, that many kinds of animals use and understand, works for everybody: stripy prey doesn't get eaten, and predators don't waste time trying to eat stuff that bites back.

Team Smells

Colors and patterns that label an animal as "one of us" or "dangerous" are fine for use in daylight, but what happens in the dark?

Poisonous tiger moths come out at night, and their main predators are bats, so they use sound to send the "Yuck! Don't eat me!" signal. When a tiger moth hears a bat's echolocation sounds, it makes a high-pitched *click*. As soon as the bat hears the click, it knows it's chasing something that won't taste very good, and turns away.

Beavers live in big family groups and don't like sharing their food or shelter with beavers that aren't family members. Inside their lodge (the living space inside the beavers' dam), it's too dark to see. So instead of a team color or pattern, beavers have a team smell. It's a mixture of the smells of all family members and can have as many as fifty different ingredients — so it's too complicated to imitate. Any beaver without the family stink will get chased out of the lodge!

Many mammals have a "team smell" that labels family members as "us" and any animal without it as "them." When your pet cat rubs its head against you, it's trading smells with you to show that you are part of its team.

Keep Out

Unlike a sound or a flash of brightly colored body, smell can keep delivering a message even when the animal that sent it is no longer there, so smell is the ideal way to say "Keep out." Instead of having to patrol the edges of its territory all the time, an animal can leave a few smelly markers like a row of **DO NOT ENTER** signs and walk away.

This method is handy for small animals with big territories to patrol, like desert iguanas. These little reptiles are each the size of a skinny pencil case and defend territories as big as half a tennis court. They manage it by squeezing blobs of smell from a row of holes on the underside of each back leg. Each blob is coated with a waxy layer to keep the smell from escaping too quickly. Unlike the desert sand around it, the wax also absorbs ultraviolet light, which iguana eyes are good at seeing, making the scent marks stand out like black beacons.

Pandas have very big, forested mountain territories. They mark trees on their borders with scent from a gland under their tails. But to send an extra signal —"The panda who left this message is very BIG indeed"— they do handstands to get their bottoms as high up the tree trunk as possible!

20

HEY! CAN'T YOU SMELL?

THIS IS PRIVA

DESERT IGUANA SQUEEZING OUT A BLOB

KEEP
OUT

ENOR-
MOUS
PANDA
LIVES
HERE!

A stale smell shows that that part of the territory isn't very well patrolled and could be a good place to invade. So animals never miss a chance to scent-mark their territories, as anyone who has ever walked a dog knows. On a thirty-minute walk, a dog may pee in ten different places, leaving a clear "This is mine!" message every time.

No Really . . . I Said "Keep Out!"

Sometimes smell just isn't enough to keep intruders at bay, and a stronger signal is needed. Wolves live in big extended family groups and back up their territorial scent marks with howling. The whole pack joins in, even the pups, to make the loudest sound possible. Neighboring packs listen carefully to one another's howls and can tell how strong another pack is from its howling, so disputes over boundaries can be settled without a fight.

Howler monkeys, too, use howling to keep out of territory trouble. Howlers live in family groups called troops, but in the dense greenery of the South and Central American rain forests where they live, keeping track of neighboring troops is tricky. This matters because if two or more troops run into one another, it can end in a nasty fight. So first thing every morning the males in each troop howl loudly to show exactly where their troop is. This is such an important part of howler-monkey life that males have a huge throat pouch, just to help them howl extra loudly.

Sing It to Win It

Male birds, too, defend their territories with sound; their songs, which seem so sweet and musical to our ears, are really saying, "Keep out or else!" to rivals and "Come to me!" to potential mates. Every time a territory owner hears another male of his species singing, he has to sing back loud and clear. If he doesn't, his mate may leave him or his territory may get taken over by another male. Singing is so important that some birds sing their songs thousands of times a day.

Even though all birdsongs are delivering the same, pretty simple message, songs can be very complicated, and every species has a different one. This is partly because of the different habitats birds live in: woodland birds tend to have lots of clear whistles in their songs, as these carry well in the still air of a forest; but birds who live in grasslands or other places with few trees have songs with short

trills, which carry best in the gusty winds of open habitats. Different species also have different songs for the same reason that butterfly fish are "labeled" in different colors — no one wants to waste time courting or fighting a member of another species, so songs need to be easy to recognize. Finally, although all birds of the same species sing the same song, individual birds sing that song in slightly different ways, so birds can tell their neighbors from new intruders.

Simply Divine

Female birds want only the best fathers for their chicks and can be very picky when choosing a mate, so for many male birds, "I am gorgeous" is a more important message to get across than "Keep out." All kinds of male birds have come up with wonderful ways to express their beauty to their females, combining flamboyant feathers, fabulous singing, and fantastic dance moves — and the most fabulous and fantastic of them all is the male superb lyrebird.

First he builds his stage, a flattened circle of dirt the size of a large table. Then he starts his song-and-dance routine: he raises his huge tail of lacy feathers like a curtain over his head, shimmying so that it shakes and shivers as he jumps around; then he sings, making his song as complicated as possible by copying, perfectly, any sounds he hears — the calls of twenty different kinds of birds, plus human sounds like car alarms, chainsaws, even camera shutters — and including them in his song.

And he'll keep the whole performance going for hours on end. It's not surprising that a successful male can attract as many as six different brides to each show, because only a really strong male could be so gorgeous for so long!

Other Ways to Say "I Am Gorgeous"

Male blue birds of paradise hang upside down while making a noise like a sewing machine to attract females.

WHIRR!

WHIRR!

OK, OK! NO NEED TO FLAP!

I GET THE MESSAGE!

Male fruit flies flash their wings in complicated semaphore to signal to their mates.

Male humpback whales sing long, complicated underwater songs to say "I'm gorgeous" and to send other messages that scientists don't yet understand.

The female red-necked phalarope mates with lots of males, so *she's* the one who says "I'm gorgeous" with her bright feathers.

Male Anna's hummingbirds do perfect dives and make a buzzing sound with their special tail feathers to look good to the girls.

Great bustards inflate their throat pouches and stick out their feathers so they look like large white balloons that can be seen for miles.

Where Are You?

It's one thing to tell your potential partner how wonderful you are, but first you have to find each other, and for some animals that can be very tricky.

Elephant-nose fish live at the bottom of rivers in West Africa, where it's far too muddy to find a mate by sight, so they use electricity. They have an organ in their tail that makes patterns and pulses of electricity that are different in males and females. If a male picks up a female's electric buzz with his electric-sensing "trunk," he'll "buzz" back at her with a typical male pattern. It's their way of saying "Where are you?" and "I'm over here!"

For a stinkbug the size of your little fingernail, finding a mate in an ordinary garden would be like a human having to search the whole state of Texas for a date. Stinkbug males make the search easier by wafting smell signals in the air. Females follow the scent to the nearest plant; then the suitor guides her to him by tapping on his leaf. The taps travel all the way through the stems and leaves of the plant until the female picks up the vibrations through her legs and taps back. By exchanging signals, they home in on each other!

Long-Distance Calls

If you are trying to find a mate, but you don't know where he or she might be, then the farther your message can travel, the better. The mole cricket makes chirrup sounds to attract a mate by rubbing the edge of its wing on its leg. Like most other cricket chirps, you can't hear them more than a couple of yards away, so the mole cricket builds a burrow and make its calls from there. The shape and size of the burrow acts like a trumpet, making the cricket's voice sound 250 times louder — loud enough, in fact, to make the ground around the burrow vibrate and the sound to be heard 2,000 feet (600 meters) away!

Sound travels four times faster in water than in air, so sound is a really good way of sending messages underwater, and lots of marine creatures use it. But high, squeaky sounds don't travel as far as low ones, so black drumfish use low, throbbing sounds to call to one another in the mating season. (Unfortunately, these fishy love songs can also travel through the walls of waterfront houses and keep people awake all night.)

The bigger you are, the easier it is to make very low sounds — so blue whales, the largest creatures on Earth, also make the lowest sounds. Their low hums travel really well through water, so they can send a "Here I am" message across an entire ocean.

33

Happy Families

The signals "Where are you?", "Come here!", and "I'm gorgeous" are enough to get males and females together to mate, but caring for offspring requires even more communication.

Sea horses, unlike most fish, are great parents; but unusually, it's the males who get pregnant. Females put their eggs in the male's brood pouch, where they stay until they are ready to pop out as tiny "sea foals." As soon as one set of babies leaves Dad's pouch, Mom is ready with a new batch of eggs. To manage this teamwork, the couple must communicate well, so they meet up every morning at dawn to dance with their tails entwined.

Most mammal mothers care for babies alone, but in the case of emperor tamarins — tiny mustachioed monkeys from South America — Mom makes sure that she has the help of two dads to care for her twin babies. When she wants a rest, she signals to the double dads by sticking out her long pink tongue; they know this means it's time for them each to take a twin.

Incubating eggs and feeding chicks is a huge job, so a mother and father bird have to be a good team, and it's essential that they keep their pair bond strong. Bird couples spend a lot of time saying "Let's stay together" by greeting, preening, and displaying to each other.

Talking to Mama

Babies may start to communicate with their parents even before they are born. Anyone who's kept chickens will tell you that chicks still in the egg start to peep to their mom a couple of days before they are ready to hatch. This tells Mom to keep sitting on the eggs because her patience will soon be rewarded!

Baby crocodiles, too, start to call "Umph, umph, umph" when they are still inside their leathery-shelled eggs, buried in mud and rotting plants. These piercing little "We're ready!" cries let all the brothers and sisters in the nest know that it's time to hatch so no one gets left behind. They also trigger help from Mom. When she hears her children's voices, she comes to the nest and helps to dig the babies free, then carries them to the water in her mouth.

Probably the most important message that babies need to give their parents is "Feed me now!" Chicks in a nest have a very simple way of doing this: they open their beaks and start cheeping as soon as a parent bird is near. To make the message extra clear, the inside of a chick's mouth is often brightly colored. This works perfectly: the parent birds find a colorful gaping beak irresistible, and they just have to put food in it.

Where's My Baby?

Feeding babies is hard work, and few animal parents want to waste effort on babies that aren't their own. Babies don't want this either — if their parents feed a stranger, they might not have enough food for their own children. So where the young of many different parents are mixed up together, parents and their babies are very careful to keep in touch and prevent any mix-ups.

Every night in the breeding season, one and a half million free-tailed bats fly from their roost under Congress Avenue Bridge in Austin, Texas, leaving their hundreds of thousands of babies behind. Each mother bat returns at least once a night to suckle her single baby, and she gives it as much as a quarter of her body weight in milk every twenty-four hours. She makes sure that this precious milk goes only to her own baby by recognizing its little squeaky contact call. A mother bat knows its baby's voice among all the thousands of others in the same area of the roof.

Fluffy gray king penguin chicks at the South Pole must make sure that when their parents come home with a meal, they can find their babies among thousands of other gray fluffy chicks huddled together for warmth. They, too, do it by voice, and can tell their parents' voices from those of all other adults, even when the howling Antarctic wind drowns out half the calls.

Goo-Goo, Ga-Ga

Baby birds don't have to learn how to "gape," and parent birds don't have to learn that it means "Feed me now!" A lot of simple animal signaling is like this, with animals born knowing how to send signals and how to understand them. But some more complicated kinds of communication — like singing, for instance — need a little practice.

Chaffinches are handsome little garden birds whose song is one of the lovely sounds of spring all over Europe. But chaffinches have to learn their song. Wild chaffinches listen to the songs of lots of other males, and then they practice very quietly, with their beaks closed. At first it's a confusing mix of too many notes, but after a few weeks of listening and practice, each male chaffinch is ready to sing his song: it's similar enough to that of other chaffinches to say *what* he is, but with enough of his own composition in to say *who* he is.

Dolphin calves click and whistle almost from birth and make a wider range of sounds than adult dolphins do. Scientists think they may be "babbling" like human babies do. From the age of about seven months, a human baby tries out all the different sounds he or she can possibly make, to see what happens. Useful sounds — like "Mama" or "Dada"— are remembered, but sounds a baby doesn't hear spoken (because they belong to a language Mom and Dad don't speak) or that don't have an effect get forgotten. After a few months, baby dolphins, too, have dropped some sounds and kept others, so both human and dolphin babies end up with a tool kit of sounds that match the grown-ups around them.

42

WORKER BEE FEEDING LARVAE

NECTAR-LOADED FLOWERS

WORKER BEES FEEDING QUEEN

PHEROMONES BEING SWAPPED

QUEEN

FORAGER BEE

WORKER BEES CLEANING UP

DANCING BEE

INSIDE A BEEHIVE

Living Together

Good communication helps mates find each other and helps parents bring up babies — and it also keeps communities working together.

Honeybees live together in colonies of up to a hundred thousand. There is usually just one queen. This queen does nothing but lay eggs. All the other bees are her children. They are mostly (female) workers that tend the queen, look after the eggs and larvae, clean out the hive, and fly off in search of nectar and pollen to keep everybody well fed. Everything is perfectly ordered because of a very clever system of chemical communication. The queen and the workers trade cocktails of chemical messages called pheromones, which control the behavior of all the bees in the colony, making sure everyone does the right job at the right time.

The bees also use dance to communicate with one another. A foraging bee that has found nectar-loaded flowers needs to tell as many other workers about it as possible so they can gather lots of nectar for the colony, so she dances, waggling her bottom as she crosses the comb inside the hive. Other bees touch her with their antennae, feeling the direction of her dance, the number of her waggles, and how excited she is. These things tell them where the nectar can be found. Then they make a "beeline" for the flowers.

THE OUTSIDE OF A BEEHIVE

Rumbles in the Jungle

African elephants also live in family groups whose survival depends on working together. When food and water are scarce, the matriarch, usually the oldest female elephant in the group, leads her group to food and water, and when predators threaten calves, the herd works together to protect them. Both rely on good communication.

THE GOOD OLD DAYS...

← THE MATRIARCH

Researchers have found that elephants use 160 touch and visual signals, and another 70 sound signals. Some of these sound signals work in an extraordinary way. Elephants make rumbling sounds well below the range of human hearing. Like all low sounds, these are very good at traveling quite far in the air, but they also travel like tiny earthquakes through the ground, so elephants can feel them with their sensitive feet and trunks. In quiet areas of Africa, elephant rumbles can call the herd together over several miles. This could certainly explain how, when part of the herd is in trouble, the rest of the gang seems to appear out of nowhere as if by magic.

Communication: The Dark Side

AN UNTRUSTWORTHY HOVERFLY

LIAR!

SNEAK!

Wherever there is communication there is also lying, and I'm sorry to have to tell you that there are some liars in the animal world. Hoverflies, for example, have the bright black and yellow stripy pattern that says "danger," just like a wasp. But hoverflies are lying: they have no sting. Similarly, milk snakes have a warning pattern of red, yellow, and black stripes, like the venomous coral snake, but milk snakes are harmless.

Milk snakes and hoverflies are using their lies in self-defense — but there are much more lethal liars. The fangblenny can make itself look and behave just like a cleaner wrasse, advertising cleaning services to reef fish. But its customers soon find out that the fangblenny is lying when it bites a chunk out of them. The female bolus spider wafts a pheromone that is exactly like the one female moths use to say, "Here I am! Come and get me." Male moths fly up eagerly, expecting a hot date, and instead end up as a spider's supper.

A SNEAKY MILK SNAKE

49

But there aren't many liars, because if this kind of lying got too common everyone would lose out. The meaning of the original message would change: a hoverfly's stripes would say "dinner," not "danger," and the fangblenny's uniform would not say "Trust me," but "Eat me before I eat you." Everyone, both liars and truth-tellers, could get eaten.

Truth and Lies

Believing a lie can get you into trouble, as we've seen from the bolus spider. A female who believes a male who lies about how big and strong he is can end up mating with a wimp; a male who believes the same lie might give up and lose a fight that he could have won. So animals are on the lookout for lies, and for honest signals that can't be faked.

Every autumn, male red deer compete to mate with the most females. Fighting with those big pointy antlers is dangerous, though, so they try to decide which of them is strongest by showing off. They roar at one another — loud, deep, long roars that say, "I'm big and fit and strong." The great thing about roaring is that it can't be faked: it's hard work, and to make a big, strong sound you have to actually be a big, strong deer. Many contests don't get further than roaring because weaker males can hear how strong the opposition is and know it's not worth risking injury in a fight. Only males that are so evenly matched that their roars sound the same settle their rivalry with a real fight.

YOU'LL HAVE TO HAVE A REAL FIGHT TO SETTLE IT...

I'm SURE I WAS LOUDER

Monkey Business

So far we've talked about messages and signals, which, like road signs, are fine for simple communication. But you couldn't have a real conversation using traffic signals. For complicated communication about ideas and feelings, places and things, you need language, and one of the first things a language needs is words. Words can be made of sounds, gestures, smells, visual displays, or anything that an animal's senses can detect. For example:

The sounds *k*, *a*, and *t* together mean CAT, and **means the same in sign language.**

The key thing is that CAT and **are always the same and always mean the same thing.**

Humans are certainly not the only ones to have words. Vervet monkeys have different alarm calls for different sorts of predators, such as eagles, snakes, and leopards. When vervets hear the "snake" call, they all stand up on their hind legs and look down at the ground, carefully watching for a slithering python. When they hear "leopard," they leap high into the trees where a leopard couldn't catch them, and when they hear "eagle," they dive into dense bushes where an eagle couldn't spot them.

Several species of African monkey have been found to have predator "words," and different species living in the same area understand one another's predator calls. This is a big advantage, since it means many more pairs of eyes looking out for danger, and many more voices raising the alarm.

But words alone aren't enough; to make a language, they need to be strung into sentences, with a more complicated meaning — and it looks as if monkeys do this too. They add other calls to the predator alarm "words," that, judging by the reaction of the troop, say things like "Right now!" or "Far away."

To try to find out what monkeys are saying, researchers record their calls, then play them back and see what the troop does. This is tricky and time-consuming, and doesn't work very well for the quieter calls that monkeys use for one-to-one communication. But if monkeys can say "Eagle up above right now!" and "Leopard quite far away — not urgent," who knows what else they might talk about? They can certainly use words to lie. A monkey that doesn't want to share a particularly yummy food item might call out "Snake, right now!" to send the rest of the troop running for the treetops, leaving the liar to eat its special food-find in peace.

← A PARTICULARLY YUMMY FOOD ITEM

SNAKE!
Right now...!

Talking Animal

Scientists and others who study language and communication argue about whether animals, like those monkeys, really have a language in the same way we do. If they do, then perhaps they could learn a bit of ours. Some researchers think that there are animals that have already learned "human."

Chimps are our closest relatives, but they don't have vocal cords, tongues, and mouths like us, so they could never form spoken words. But their hands and many of the gestures they use are very like ours, so in the 1960s an experiment was begun to teach a young chimp, which her human caretakers named Washoe, American Sign Language. Washoe learned 250 different signs. She also taught another chimp 50 signs without any human help at all. Washoe could make sentences asking for food, play, or drink, and would put signs together to help name or describe things she'd never seen before. The other captive chimps in her group used normal chimp sounds, gestures, and touch to communicate with one another, but also used human sign language.

Parrots are wonderful mimics, so it's easy for them to say human words, but Alex, an African gray parrot that lived with researcher Irene Pepperberg for thirty years, seemed to *understand* the 150 words he learned to say. Alex could answer questions about the shape, color, size, and number of objects placed before him, even when he'd never seen them before. Like Washoe, Alex sometimes made sentences on his own that seemed to show that he really understood the words he was using; when Irene once had to leave him at the vet for treatment, he said, "Come here. I love you. I'm sorry. I want to go back."

Some people say that Washoe and Alex didn't really understand what they were saying and that their words tell us nothing about animal thoughts and feelings. But Washoe and Alex were both far from their wild homes, living with humans, not their own kind. That's like you or me learning "alien" in a flying saucer on the way to Mars, and I wonder how well we'd manage? Our human language has evolved over tens of thousands of years to express what goes on in our world, in our heads, and in our hearts. But animals are not people; they have their own thoughts and feelings that are very different from ours. How could our words ever fully express what they might want to say?

Scientists listening out for alien communications from space have developed computer programs that can spot the tell-tale footprint of a language in any signal. One day this technique could be used on dolphin sounds, which might be close to our idea of language. Maybe then we'll finally know what animals have to say about us.

58

Index

60

Glossary

colony – a group of animals that live together and share the jobs they need to do to stay alive

echolocation – the use of sounds made by bats and some other animals to create echoes that the animal can use to find its way around

evolution – how animals and plants change over many generations, sometimes enough to become whole new species

habitat – the kind of place where you would find a particular animal. For example, a whale's habitat is the ocean, not the forest.

incubating – occurs when birds sit on their eggs to keep them warm so the chicks inside can grow. Reptiles incubate their eggs too, by burying them somewhere warm or keeping them inside their bodies.

matriarch – the female leader of a group of animals, usually older and wiser than the others; a kind of super granny!

pheromones – a signal-carrying chemical produced by an animal, that prompts a particular behavior when sensed by other members of its species

semaphore – a type of signaling using flags held in different positions to convey letters and words. Fruit flies hold their wings in different positions to send messages, too.

species – a specific kind of animal or plant. A dandelion is a species of plant and a zebra is a species of animal.

territory – the area an animal uses to find food, shelter, and mates and doesn't want to share with others!

toxins – another word for *poisons*

ultraviolet – a kind of light, just beyond blue in the rainbow, that humans can't see very well but insects and other animals can. It's the part of sunlight that makes you tan.

61

THAT'S ME

BOO YAKKA

SUN-O CREAM